HowExpert Gı
Dance and Chor̶ꞁ̶ꞁ̶

101 Tips to Learn How to Dance, Improve Your Choreography Skills, and Become a Better Performer

HowExpert with Sydney Skipper

Copyright HowExpert™
www.HowExpert.com

For more tips related to this topic, visit HowExpert.com/dance

Recommended Resources

- HowExpert.com – Quick 'How To' Guides on All Topics from A to Z by Everyday Experts.
- HowExpert.com/free – Free HowExpert Email Newsletter.
- HowExpert.com/books – HowExpert Books
- HowExpert.com/courses – HowExpert Courses
- HowExpert.com/clothing – HowExpert Clothing
- HowExpert.com/membership – HowExpert Membership Site
- HowExpert.com/affiliates – HowExpert Affiliate Program
- HowExpert.com/jobs – HowExpert Jobs
- HowExpert.com/writers – Write About Your #1 Passion/Knowledge/Expertise & Become a HowExpert Author.
- HowExpert.com/resources – Additional HowExpert Recommended Resources
- YouTube.com/HowExpert – Subscribe to HowExpert YouTube.
- Instagram.com/HowExpert – Follow HowExpert on Instagram.
- Facebook.com/HowExpert – Follow HowExpert on Facebook.
- TikTok.com/@HowExpert – Follow HowExpert on TikTok.

Publisher's Foreword

Dear HowExpert Reader,

HowExpert publishes quick 'how to' guides on all topics from A to Z by everyday experts.

At HowExpert, our mission is to discover, empower, and maximize everyday people's talents to ultimately make a positive impact in the world for all topics from A to Z...one everyday expert at a time!

All of our HowExpert guides are written by everyday people just like you and me, who have a passion, knowledge, and expertise for a specific topic.

We take great pride in selecting everyday experts who have a passion, real-life experience in a topic, and excellent writing skills to teach you about the topic you are also passionate about and eager to learn.

We hope you get a lot of value from our HowExpert guides, and it can make a positive impact on your life in some way. All of our readers, including you, help us continue living our mission of positively impacting the world for all spheres of influences from A to Z.

If you enjoyed one of our HowExpert guides, then please take a moment to send us your feedback from wherever you got this book.

Thank you, and we wish you all the best in all aspects of life.

Sincerely,

BJ Min
Founder & Publisher of HowExpert
HowExpert.com

PS...If you are also interested in becoming a HowExpert author, then please visit our website at HowExpert.com/writers. Thank you & again, all the best!

Table of Contents

Chapter 1: The Fundamentals

Tip 1: Why you need inspiration

Inspiration plays a role in one of the beginning steps to learning how to dance. It creates your motives for wanting to be a dancer, and it helps you identify what style of dance you may lean towards. It gets you asking the question, why do I want to become a dancer? Your inspiration doesn't just factor into your reasons for choosing to dance. As you become a more mature dancer and choreographer, the inspiration behind the piece becomes the foundation. For example, let's say a choreographer wanted to do a piece about mental health awareness. They would not just make moves or choose a random song with a good beat; they would apply research, taking inspiration from people's experiences. Maybe look at another piece that did a similar topic and apply that to their thought process in creating their work. It is only one example of how inspiration can be transitioned from the stages of a beginner dancer to a more advanced dancer.

Tip 2: Finding your inspiration

How does inspiration help you to get started? We can start by asking ourselves the same question from above: why do you want to dance? There could be a specific person who inspires you to dance, or it could be the feeling you get when you dance. The important thing is finding that inspiration for doing what you do. It gives you a reason to get started and reminds you to keep going as you develop into a stronger dancer.

Once you have identified why you want to dance or where the inspiration comes from, you can ask yourself the questions: how does that connect to me specifically in dance and not any other art or sport? Does it inspire my specific movements in the way I move like a dancer? For example, a well-known choreographer named Matt Steffanina has inspired many people to dance. Specifically, they loved his style in dance and how he focused on isolations and movements of the hand and leg, making the minor details so clean and precise.

What about your person or thing makes it an inspiration to you?

Tip 3: On the dance floor

You are taking the inspiration to the dance floor. Continuing the example of Matt Steffanina being your inspiration, what does that look like when you want to start dancing? You may want to begin by watching him dance or learning from him through videos. YouTube is a great way to find videos and watch the choreographer go through tutorials of a combo. Another recommended option, if accessible, is taking his class. In this example, you are physically learning from the person that inspires you to dance. It gets you up, moving and dancing, and constantly plugs you into what or who inspires you.

Let us go the route that the feeling you get while dancing is what inspires you. In this approach, improv is a good starting place. Turning on some of your favorite tunes that you can connect with and dancing gets you plugged into your inspiration and on your feet moving. So you go from reading, thinking, and talking about dance to diving right in and applying it to your body. Improv can be tricky, as it is something many dancers can struggle with. There is this idea that you have to know what you're doing all the time. However, in improv, you dance as you go. A common issue is getting into your head too much and overthinking your moves to the point where you are not connecting with the music. If the feeling of dance is your inspiration, feeling the music and being connected at that moment specifically is where you want to be.

Tip 4: Warming up

There is a lot of pressure put on our bodies as dancers. From the beginning, it is crucial to establish a routine of taking care of your body and fully stretching before doing any movement. You should loosen everything from stretching your neck and shoulders down to your ankles. Properly warming up doesn't just prevent injuries, but it helps us become better dancers. For example, let's say we have a dancer who is strongly suited in contemporary. In this dance style, there is a lot of leg strength and control needed to slow movements down. A dancer could work towards several beginner and advanced modern skills, including maintaining flexibility, gaining flexibility, or maintaining and developing more strength. Below we have Some tips on warming up and recommended stretches.

Tip 5: Stretches

The neck: First, you would want to make sure your legs are shoulder-width apart, then you wish to bring your chin down to touch your chest and hold for 5 seconds. Then you will tilt your head to the side, trying to touch your left ear to your left shoulder for 5 seconds. You will then tilt your head back to look at the sky or the ceiling for 5 seconds. Lastly, you will tilt your head to the right trying to touch your right ear to your right shoulder and hold for 5 seconds. You can do this around in a circle 2x

Fold overstretches: With your feet and legs together, you will slowly fold your body, reaching your hands down to touch your toes or trying to touch your nose down to your knees. To make this stretch more challenging, you can wrap your arms around your ankles and slowly pull your body closer to your legs.

Arm Circles: First, start with your right arm circling it backward 10x and then the same but forwards. You are going to do that same thing with your left arm and can do this a total of 2x

Lunge: You will make a right lunge, having one hand on each side of your leg touching the ground. The goal for this stretch is to stretch your hamstring. As you push your right lunge, the left leg behind you should remain straight, not bent, touching the ground. This will apply as well when you are making your left lunge. You can hold this stretch for about 30 seconds and switch sides.

Knee-to-chest: You can do this stretch lying down or standing up. If you are lying down, you will be flat on your back. You will then raise one leg bringing your knee to your chest. Your hands should be wrapped around your knee, pulling it closer to your chest. While stretching, you want to look out for the bottom leg you are not pulling. It should be lying flat on the ground. Try not to let the back of the knee and or leg raise from the floor while pulling your other leg up. You will hold this stretch for 30 seconds and switch legs.

In-motion: Above are some stretches that are done standing still. To get our body moving more, we will want to do some in-motion exercises, such as jumping jacks and high knees. You can do it before or after your stationary stretches to get your blood flowing.

The overall tip on warming up is to stretch everything, taking the time needed to stretch all the tiny muscles from head to toe rather than leaving the studio or finishing dancing with an injury. Another vital tip is not to dance without warming up prior; just like any sport, doing the activity before warming up leads to a vast possibility of injuries and problems down the line. Warming up does not always need to be stationary; I've been in several classes where we do jumping jacks and high knees to get the blood flowing before we even start the stationary stretching. So it doesn't look the same each day. You need to listen to your body and what it is telling you. Maybe on Sundays, your legs are tighter than others. Then you want to work on stretching the specific areas that are tighter; that is where you want to be aware of injuries that can happen, so be mindful of your body, listen to what it tells you and take care of yourself for the sake of your passion and dance and the safe of injuries.

Tip 6: *Improving your body movements*

On top of stretching and warming up properly, there should also be some areas of you pushing yourself flexibility-wise. Let's say reaching down and touching your toes has become too easy for you. Now try and push yourself to have your nose contact your knees. If we are doing lunges and find that's too easy, we can work our way down to do a split. In dance, there are always ways you can push yourself to be better. Maintaining and gaining in dance comes along with taking care of the body.

Imagine dancing for a while, and you are ready to move from a beginner contemporary class to an intermediate class. However, you are asked to do a skill you have never done, are not properly warmed up for, or have the flexibility to do. Potential injuries can come from doing a skill you are not ready to do. No matter what level you are at, protecting your body and taking care of your body is key to development as a dancer.

An example of how you can take care of your body is making sure you have a strong enough releve and core to carry yourself in a pirouette turn. For example, you are in ballet and want to do a double pirouette. However, you keep falling after your single because you do not have the core strength to stay balanced, or you can't stay on reliving to get around a second time. To prepare to do this skill, you may want to do specific exercises to train your calves and core in addition to striving for this turn.

Now that we talked about warming up, maintaining, and improving body movements. Here are some recommendations for strengthening oneself for specific skills and furthering flexibility.

Tip 7: Strengthen

Abs: Planks, crunches, and pulses are a huge recommendation. A suggestion on how to do it is to alternate between the three and work your way up to doing it for a whole song without stopping. For example, hold a plank for a minute, then immediately roll into crunches for 30, pulses for 30, and then back to a plank. It will be extremely challenging at first especially doing it to the length of a 3 minute or longer song. However, doing it to the beat of the music helps you stay on beat and can help you train to hear the musicality within songs.

Calves: Releve and eleve are the main exercises that focus on the calves. These may also be known as calf raises, but first, the difference between releve and eleve. Releve is a French term meaning to raise up; this would look like you have your feet in the first position. Next, you will slowly raise up to releve and slowly lower back down from a plie position. You can start doing this with both feet and then work your way to doing one leg at a time. Now when it comes to eleve, this means the dancer will rise to the balls of their feet without a plie and it will be on a straight leg. You can specifically work on balance and using your core to keep your center in this one.

Tip 8: Identifying your dance style

Types of dance styles and an introduction to them.

Ballet: This form of dance helps influence other types of dances. Classical and nonclassical ballet emphasizes graceful expressions done, in some cases, on pointe.

14

Tap: This style heavily focuses on your feet and uses them to create rhythmic patterns. It requires special shoes that have a metal plate on the bottom to be used to produce sound.

Jazz: This type of dance involves a lot of originality, and a difference you will see in this type of style is it is a bit more dramatic with the body movements.

Contemporary: This style is in between ballet and modern. It does not stick to grace movements like ballet but is not as rebellious as modern. It has the technique of ballet and uses that to create more movements. Contemporary does have more to it than modern, and it focuses on connecting the mind to the body and showing that.

Modern: This style does not focus on the traditional ballet movements but focuses on expressions and storytelling of one's inner feelings and thoughts. This style emphasizes expression and shows that through moves.

Jazz-funk: A Jazz-funk class combines jazz and funk; it takes the fundamentals of jazz and the backbeat of some groove.

Hip hop: Originally emerged from jazz and street styles. Within hip hop, there are specific categories such as jerkin, popping, locking, and breakdance. Hip hop was originally seen on the streets of New York, where battles would form between dancers and crews.

Tip 9: Your style

The next step includes finding your style. To learn how to dance, you want to know what type of dance you are trying to learn. For example, is it ballet, modern, jazz, hip hop, contemporary, cultural, etc.? Having a specific goal for what type of dance you want to learn will help you when it comes to other steps in the beginning process.

For example, say your dance style is hip hop; your inspiration can come from a specific hip hop dancer you watched or are watching. It can come from music; maybe hip hop and rap music are your things. When it comes to fundamentals, you can learn the basics specifically dedicated to your dance style. You will know to shoot for beginner hip hop classes instead of jazz-funk when officially starting classes.

Identifying one's style doesn't just stop at what type of dance you do but is also used when you are further down the line as a dancer when learning combos. Your style helps you when it comes to making choices on the dance floor. What I mean by style and choices is that once you have learned a piece or a combo you want to perform, make it yours and unique.

Suppose we have three dancers that are in a jazz-funk class. They just finished their combo and are about to run it all the way through. You want to get to a certain point where you stop thinking about what moves come first and last and start thinking about how you want to present it. Your choices, maybe one dance, might change some of the combos to make them more fitting and comfortable. Another dancer might hit specific moves harder and faster, and another move slower to different levels within the piece. The third person might stick to how the work is taught. All three show the same work together when it comes to performing, but each person looks slightly different because they made their own choices and have their own style on the combo.

Tip 10: Understanding the fundamentals

Whether or not your type is hip hop, jazz, or ballet, you need to understand the fundamentals and terminologies. I have been in hip-hop classes when the instructor teaches the combo and references ballet terminology to demonstrate and explain a move.

In fundamentals, we are talking about ballet terminology and basics in the specific dance style you are leaning toward. Where you can learn and improve fundamentals are technique classes. In these classes, you are not learning a combo but are working on skills, strengthening oneself to become a better dancer.

Some key examples of ballet fundamentals you should understand are the ballet positions and the difference between the first position and fifth position. Then, you would go through the different dance styles and learn the fundamentals of each type.

Tip 11: Rhythm and finding your beat

Rhythm is not something everyone immediately has; however, there are ways you can work on finding the rhythm and beats within music and learn to translate that to your body as you become a dancer. My first tip would be to study music. Listen to music and try to identify the base of different instruments within the songs and the sounds and beats they make. Try picking a song and listening to it multiple times. You might be able to hear a background beat the 5th time you've heard the music that you did not hear the first time around.

 Next, I would recommend practicing 8-counts within the song. You counting that out loud represents your body and the movements you will make to the song's beats. Try this with a variety of different music. You will begin to notice some pieces 8-counts will be a lot faster than others and some common trends within the songs. For example, Michael Jackson's song Billie Jean has a constant 8-count throughout his piece with a fast tempo; if we look at Justin Timberlake's Mirrors, the 8-counts are a lot slower than Michael Jackson's song but are also constant. However, if we look at Missy Elliot's song Lose Control, this song has several opportunities where the beat speeds up, slows down, and even pauses. You can dance to all these songs, and you just need to identify the rhythm and tempo and match that with your body as you dance.

 The last tip would be improv. Now that you hear the music and can identify the tempo and beat, it is time to match your body to the 8-counts in the song. Something fundamental with improv, especially for beginners, is not to care about what you look like but portray how you feel. Whether you are full-out crunking it or doing side steps, the key point here is staying on the beat to find your rhythm. Improv is not about looking the best but rather just showing who you are. As you become a better dancer, improv can become more challenging when trying more intricate moves and pushing yourself more. However, for now, the combination of listening, identifying, and moving will help you become a dancer. Like any sport, repetition is key for muscle memory and overall improvement.

To get better at finding the rhythm, practice these steps consistently. Repeatedly listening to music helps you to be able to identify beats that may be hard to hear. As you continue to practice 8-counts over time, you will be able to add and count in between with lots of practice. Improv more consistently, and not only will you be dancing more on the beat, but you will also become more confident with dancing in general.

Summary

Overall, the fundamentals you want to be aware of is finding that inspiration. Knowing why you dance will help you be a better dancer and be motivated to practice dancing every day. Next, you always want to take care of your body. You should be warming up and stretching every single time you dance; choosing to dance without thoroughly warming up could lead to several injuries that we want to avoid. Next, you want to identify your dance style, what type of dance you want to work on right now, and what style you are interested in. Once you know what style you're going for, you can then move on to finding your rhythm and beat. Finding your rhythm is about having fun with the music and listening and dancing to music to get you in the feel of dancing without the pressure of choreography, classes, and other people watching.

Chapter 2: Classes

Tip 12: Technique classes

No matter what type of dance you do, foundational technique classes are always needed. First, we will look at what technique classes are compared to other courses. Technique classes focus on the foundations of the style of dance. For example, ballet would be a ballet technique, focusing on the five positions: first, second, third, fourth, and fifth. **Eleve** and **releve**: where should your balance be? Are you on the sides of your feet or the balls of your feet? **Plie**: have you turned out while you plie, or do you turn out? **Develope**: are your hips turned out? Are your legs straight? **Passe**: how high is your passe? These are all essential things to learn as you become a dancer, and here is why.

Let's say you go straight into ballet combos without learning and the foundations. That way, there will be a lot of bad habits forming. For example, let's say you are doing pique turns across the floor; your passe is very low, and your releve is on the outside of your feet. This way, you are improperly balanced, so you end up falling when you try to do pique turns across the floor. Continuing the example, let's say as you notice yourself slipping, instead of fixing it, you try it more, and you just continue to do pique turns in plier wets. The problem here is muscle memory. Your muscles will remember to releve on the outside of your foot instead of the balls your foot, making it a bad habit that you continually do while you dance. So as you become a better dancer, you have to backtrack to fix your bad habits before moving on to stronger skills.

Technique classes aren't just something you do at the beginning of dance but throughout your dance journey. For example, we talked about skipping techniques and watching bad habits limit your dancing. But bad habits can also form as you go through classes, even after learning techniques. So technique classes are not just one and done but need to be something you continue to take, so your muscles don't develop bad habits.

Another reason why you need technique classes is for terminology. The teacher may not always demonstrate what he asks us to do in combo classes or other classes. For example, a teacher may say, across the floor, we will do two pique turns into a fan kick into an illusion. If your teacher said that, would you understand what he is saying? Would you know what to do physically? I have personally been in beginner hip hop classes where the teacher will use ballet terminology and not demonstrate to see if we know ballet terminology. So ballet terminology is not just used in ballet classes, and the same goes for any other technique and terminology. The languages and styles in dance cross each other; you will find ballet in jazz and jazz in hip hop, etc. Some examples of technique classes are ballet technique and jazz technique.

Tip 13: First ballet technique

As a beginner, I recommend taking ballet technique classes, as ballet is the foundation in almost all dance styles.

Doing technique classes is like starting at level 1; it is the foundation needed before moving to level 2. Therefore, dancers of all ages, styles, and skill levels need technique classes.

Tip 14: Combo classes

You are beginning combo classes or classes where a choreographer will teach you a piece, and you will learn it within about an hour and perform it. These classes are essential because they get you to learn choreography from a choreographer. It gets you practicing different combos and is one of the strongest ways to push you to be a dancer. There are some things you can expect when it comes to class. The teacher will normally lead a warm-up for about 15 to 20 minutes, and then we get into the combo.

As you take my classes, you'll begin to realize that they are different because I'll go first move at a different pace. For example, some teachers will teach a good portion of the combo and then play the music, while others will demonstrate the combo first and then start the choreography, and then we have some teachers who will teach about one or two counts then play the music. So as you take more classes, you must figure out what teaching style works best for you. A beginner class is a great starting place because it's at a slower pace easier for people to pick up than intermediate-advanced classes.

Tip 14: Beginner musicality

Beginner classes are on the simpler end. You will not be hitting moves too fast as a beginner dancer, and the timing will typically be on the easier side and very simple to identify. However, as you grow into the more advanced and intermediate classes, the classes won't be as easy, the choreography will be more complex, the musicality will be very challenging to hear, and counts will be applied to speed up the pace in choreography and the class.

Tip 15: Identifying classes

Where can you find these classes? You can look up dance studios within your area and consider the courses they offer there. You can also look online. I know there are options: you can take online dance classes or go to YouTube and find tutorials for beginner combos. However, I highly recommend you get in the studio; that way, if you have any questions, you can ask them directly. There is also good energy from being in the studio compared to dancing alone at home.

Why do you need these classes? These classes are necessary for you to learn how to pick up choreography, but it also gives you a piece to go home and practice. For example, let's say you are in the beginning hip-hop class and you're struggling with the combo. You could always record the choreographer doing it and practice it at home. This is when the repetition plays into muscle memory, and you can work on picking up choreography faster.

Tip 16: Connections

Combo classes are where you can meet other dancers who are in the same boat as you. I have met people who have been dancing since they were 5 to people who have been dancing for three months. Meeting other dancers is a huge way to help your progress as a dancer; they may have tips on picking up choreo faster. In addition, you can meet people you can practice the piece with and discover other choreographers by meeting other dancers. Learning to dance with a group of people or even just one other person may motivate you more than learning by yourself.

Some tips I have for as you take combo classes is to start at the beginner level. If you are nervous, maybe bring a friend with you and use the time to focus on yourself and not other people. If you are physically in class, it's so easy to compare yourself to other dancers. Still, your focus is on them and not yourself while you are doing that. At that point, you're not necessarily picking up choreography or rhythm to make yourself a better dancer, and the class just becomes a period of comparison. You must be focused and present while in class if you want to get the best from it.

Tip 17: Repetition

Repetition is vital for memorizing choreography and gaining skills when becoming a dancer. This chapter will look at what repetition looks like in dance. What it benefits, and some ways you can do repetition to help you become a better dancer.

Repetition in dance can be as simple as stretching daily. It is doing the things necessary for you to be a better dancer on a daily basis, not a weekly basis. Working on your technique, flexibility, and strength daily. When it comes to combos, if you are first learning a combo to get it into your brain, you will need to run it through repeatedly to get it into your brain and your body. Taking that combo home with you and running it through repeatedly until you can nail it works on muscle memory. You can remember the combo in your body without thinking about what moves comes next.

As we talked about above regarding your muscle memory, repetition also benefits your flexibility and strength. After stretching repetitively, you will see a difference in your flexibility. Maybe you can now touch the ground or your toes when folding your stretch, perhaps you are closer, or you can finally do a split. You can do repetition by exercising or stretching multiple times a day. For example, instead of just once a day, you could do releve in the morning, during lunch, and in the evening for a total of three times a day.

The same thing applies when you are learning a combo, you don't want just to review it in one sitting but rather really test to see if you know the dance by taking a break from it, taking your mind off of it, and coming back to the song to see if you can still remember it. So we have exercises, stretching, and learning combos multiple times throughout the day. Overall we are just dancing daily. If you want to become a better dancer, you need to dance frequently. Meaning any free time that you have, whatever is the simplest things such as step touches or practicing a combo that you learned, the only way you're going to get better is through repetition and practicing on your own.

How repetition helps you in the future will be in the habit of stretching daily, which is an excellent habit to have as a dancer. In addition, you will be in the practice of setting aside time multiple times throughout the day to focus on your craft. Hopefully, with a constant rehearsal of learning combos and reviewing them, you will be able to pick up choreography a bit quicker as your body will be used to specific moves that you have been practicing. No matter what level you're at, dance repetition seems to help improve dancers in all aspects.

Tip 18: Observation

Observation of dancers, this is a very overlooked step I would say that really benefits you when becoming a dancer. Now there's a difference between observing dancers and wanting to learn from them and observing dancers more comparably. Observing and training with more advanced dancers forces you and pushes you to be more focused, more present, and to spend time working on your craft outside of the studio on your own time. It is something really easy to do. It can be observing dancers in the studio or splitting into groups when you're performing your combo to see how they hit things differently from you, seeing what flavors they add to the choreography and how they make it unique to them. Then there could be you observing dancers off YouTube, watching professional dancers and beginner dancers, seeing something they might have in common in how they perform.

When you observe dancers, it's more than just watching how they move; but it's also following their lifestyle, who they train with, how they train their inspiration and applying that to yourself. So let's just say there is a choreographer you want to work with; what you would do is look at dancers who train with that choreographer and observe what classes they take. If you want to get to a specific level of dancing, you will see how many hours they spend working on their craft at home versus in the studio, who inspires them, and what motivates them, and then you apply that yourself and your craft.

How does the observation benefit you? If you observe the correct way others dance, you will be able to hit beats that you didn't necessarily hear the first time? I've personally been in classes, and when we're split into groups, other dancers I have watched have hit beats within the music that I didn't necessarily hear at first until I watched them before me. Then moving to my performance, I was able to apply what I learned and listen to the music better, and hit those beats stronger than previously.

Observing helps you in the sense of setting a goal. You can watch a specific dancer over the years, observe them, and make them your inspiration by applying their dance style; it helps you make a goal as to where you want to be as a dancer. The goal gives you something to work towards every day and can even be part of your motivation for dancing. Observing and looking up to dancers helps you stay motivated; it gets you in a sort of routine. As for training-wise, if you want to dance like this dancer, learning to train in similar styles and learning to train with certain people pushes you to get more involved in the dance environment and be a better performer.

When you observe other dancers, something you can also look for is not just how they're hitting the moves and how they make them unique to them, but the performance that they give makes you excited to watch them. Do they have facials that draw you in, attitude, or storytelling, and if so, how can you take what you're watching and apply it to yourself? It's very easy to get caught up in the game of comparing how they can perform or dance so well or be so talented that I want to be like them. Instead of looking at them and saying, wow, I really like the choices that made their performance exciting to watch, how can I create my own performance in a way that I'm just as exciting to watch. So not comparing yourself in a way that hurts you or criticizes you but in a way that can uplift you and push you to be a stronger dancer, not looking at them and saying, oh wow, they're so great.

I'm looking at them and saying they have qualities within their dance that I would like to work towards. How can I learn from them? How can I watch their performance and apply that to my dancing to become a better performer? Once you get in the mindset of comparison, it pushes you down as an artist or a creator because then you're constantly comparing your work to others. It's going to be even harder for you to feel comfortable making the choices you need to make or to play around with facials to figure out how you want to perform the piece. But learning to observe other people's art and beauty and complement them without questioning your own craft is a necessary skill to have when trying to develop yourself as a stronger dancer.

Tip 19: Character

Learning how to dance is finding what makes you who you are! You can also see characters used in dancing by taking on a persona and telling a story. For example, let's say you are in a contemporary class, and the piece is about losing a loved one. You can enhance your performance by adding emotions to your face. You can develop the feeling from a personal experience, and you share a part of yourself through that. Or by taking on the character of someone who lost their loved ones. So I guess you can say some acting comes into play when it comes to performance. However, for the beginning stages, we are going to look at facials and finding yourself within your dancing.

Tip 20: Expression

Demonstrating the character within your moves does not necessarily mean being 100% at all moments. Maybe you can subtly hit movements at specific moments and pop out in other moments within the combo. It is a smart choice, and experimenting with how you want to perform this, if you want to make this move a little smaller so that way the next move pops out really big and grabs the audience's attention, you have the freedom to do that with your character as a dancer. So your performance, character, choices, and facials all go hand-in-hand, making you a stronger and more exciting performer.

Being a good dancer or a better dancer isn't just about how well you can execute these moves, but how you can combine all of it to perform to the audience and gather their attention. You can be the best dancer and have the most technique and be able to do all these tricks, but if you don't figure out who your character is or are not able to use your facials and expression to perform, you may not be as entertaining to watch.

Facials: most dancers choose to add facials after learning the choreography; however, another way to add it is while learning choreography. That way, it's like a muscle memory thing; when you hit a specific move, your facials automatically go with it.

You are making the piece fit you. Another suggestion for making a combo or a piece more you is understanding the music and feeling it without dancing to it. If you can connect with the music and the story, the performance part will be there, and the choreography will follow right after.

Summary

So there are several different types of classes you can take. The best classes for beginners are technique classes, mainly focusing on ballet because ballet is the foundation for all dance styles. However, there are also classes like jazz technique. Technique classes are something that you should not take only once and be done but should be something you continue to take as you go through your dance journey. The next step for you would be a beginner combo class. This class would be any style you were interested in but will challenge you in the sense of picking up choreography and getting the movement from your brains to your body in alignment with the music. One of the key things to getting your body to remember the dance moves is repetition; whether you are in the class doing it over and over again or if you take the piece home to practice it, you'll become better at dancing the more you practice it. Next, it would be observing other dancers; watching the way they move can help us as dancers pick out things that they like and hear beats musicality-wise that we weren't able to hear before. The last step would be finding your character, having fun within the peace, and telling a story about your performance.

Chapter 3: Improvement

Tip 21: Film

So you have been dancing for a bit, or you are at the stage where you are ready to improve your dancing. The first step into improving your dancing is to film yourself dancing. You need to see yourself dance to see what area you want to improve. It is good to have a film of yourself to witness your growth as a dancer, compare your dancing in your beginner stages to the level you are at now, critique your dancing that you are currently at, and set a goal of where you are would like to be.

Where to get the film? Nowadays, several combo classes section out 15 min windows just for filming and to get you to perform in groups. It is an excellent opportunity to have captured film and practice performing in front of a camera. Also, working in groups gets you dancing in other dancers' practicing spacing. Another way you can get film is just by filming yourself at home with your phone. It does not need to be in class, but sometimes filming at home with just yourself is one of the best ways to perform and be the most confident within yourself.

Tip 22: Study your dancing

Watching yourself dance: you want to watch yourself perform now that you have some footage. Something I look for is, are my facials visible? Am I hitting specific moves the best I can? Am I going full out? It's the tiniest things in one's performance that can make a huge difference. So when watching yourself, you want to critique yourself to see what areas you want to focus and work on. In addition to protecting yourself, it is really good to watch other dancers. If your film is of you in a group, watch the other dancers and study that too. Each of you is doing the same choreography but has your own twist on it. Watch how other dancers translate and perform their moves. They may hit something that you really like, or another dancer looks cleaner when they do this combo. It gives you something to shoot for and work on.

Specifically, filming and watching yourself dance on film is good at showing your facials and storytelling. It is really easy for dancers to dance and make the moves; however, the challenge comes in when you add the attitude and the facials, forcing you to multitask and still remember the choreography. Watching yourself on film does an excellent job at showing if you portrayed that story. If you told the story, are you entertaining and exciting to watch, or are you just good at completing the moves? Or are you more dancing the choreo how it's taught while having a blank face. Dancing requires a lot of movement, not just in your body but your face, the way you portray it, the way you carry yourself, how you hit this move, and make it unique to you. When you watch yourself perform, you should have an exciting feeling, seeing yourself give everything you have and portraying those facials that serve looks and bring the story to life.

Tip 23: Collaboration with other dancers

Collaborating with other dancers pushes your work ethic, challenges your performance, and can add to your inspiration. Surrounding yourself with other dancers puts you in an environment where you can challenge each other to work in your craft daily and behave like an accountability partner. How does that benefit you? Just like working, having someone there will push you. You can even teach with an assistant by learning a combo with other dancers or creating a combo with other dancers, then watching other dancers perform and critiquing each other.

Tip 24: Improv

Improv is an essential part of your development as a dancer because it allows you to challenge your creativity. It gets you more connected to your dance in the form of an expression rather than just something to do physically. There are several different ways to dance improv: to music, with the image in your head of creating shapes or feeling a space, or with other people to bounce off of each other's energy and creativity. In addition, improv helps you as a choreographer when coming up with moves. Sometimes you get to a point where you get stuck, and to get past that, you can just play the music, do what you've already choreographed, and then see what naturally comes next.

Improv is a great place to start choreography.

When you're new to choreographing things, it can be challenging to figure out where to start, so playing the music and just letting loose with it gets you flying with movements that come naturally and flowing with ideas and can help you get the choreography moving. You can also challenge yourself as an improv dancer. To develop yourself as a dancer, you want to stay away from making the same moves over and over again, so when you're doing improv, do something that comes naturally. Still, if you are repeating the same movement, that is an excellent place to develop. You can mess around and try new activities and new inspirations and apply that to your improv. For example, let's say you're improving, but you're using a specific body part to lead you; let's just say your head is guiding you through this. You would start dancing from your head and let that flow through your body. There should be unfamiliar movements within that, so it will be a challenge for you because it is something you've never done before. You can mess around with it, and it doesn't just have to be your head; it can be your shoulders leading you, your leg, or your arm.

Tip 25: Storytelling

The next step to being a better dancer is using facials and storytelling to enhance your dance. Your performance should not just be about the moves you do and how quickly you can hit them, how strong you can hit them, etc., but it should be about telling a story and expressing it. Facials require your mind to focus on things other than just the movement and don't come naturally to every dancer. Sometimes, when you're trying to concentrate on facials, it challenges you as a dancer to a certain extent in that you don't have to focus on it as much as you can focus on something else. A major area where dancers struggle is knowing when to use facials, how to use facials, and just remembering to do so.

Tip 26: Practicing facials

A tip that I have for dancers trying to work on their facials is practicing facials in the mirror. You can do this to your favorite song just by exploring with it. It's easier to practice something you're unfamiliar with when you're by yourself rather than in the dance class in front of a bunch of people. You can do facials by scenarios, so let's say someone wants to be sassy; you can also practice the facials of someone more scared or happy. There are several different emotions that you can practice in the mirror.

Tip 27: Combining facials and choreography

Now where it gets difficult is multitasking doing both facials and dancing. A tip I have for adding facials to your choreo is learning the facials or making the facials as you are learning the choreography so that they become almost like a dance move to you. You remember choreography by practicing it over and over and running it to music. So just like you would do any other dance, practice the facials over and over and apply it to the choreography.

A way that might help you remember it is to learn to do the facials while learning the choreography. That way, the facials you do at specific parts or with specific moves automatically go with the choreography you are learning.

Back on the topic of storytelling, we just went over facials. Another way you can challenge yourself as a dancer is by using your choreography to tell a story. It is a huge challenge that you can take on and does require research. For example, let's say you're doing a piece about the musical Hairspray; you would want to research to see what time this takes place. We know that it takes place in the 60s, so what are some dance moves that were popular then that we can incorporate into our choreography today? What type of costumes or hairstyles, how is their posture, how do they talk, how did they walk? All these little details help us tell the story and use dance to help incorporate our storytelling.

So now we have different ways you can challenge yourself as a dancer. As a choreographer, we can work on facials and apply the storytelling to your performance. Specifically, I can see what you're doing and ensure each movement attributes to the research. You got to motivate us or be our inspiration when we create a piece with a story to be told through it.

Tip 28: Challenging choreography

The next step we can look at is challenging yourself in classes. Let's say you've been doing beginner choreography and hip-hop, and it's getting to a point where the choreography is getting easy to you. You're picking up the choreography faster. You have the freedom of adding your facial and making your own choices. However, the class is not challenging to you anymore; at this point, we would want to start to look at intermediate courses. Intermediate classes challenge you in choreography and musicality, performance, and focusing on the details. Sometimes you may be ready to advance into an intermediate course in one specific dance genre but not the other, and that is OK. What I mean by that is you may be ready to go into intermediate hip-hop but still need to be in a beginner contemporary class. There is no set time it takes for someone to outgrow a course or level. So if you were taking studio classes and feel ready to move on to the next level up because it challenges you, then that is the steps you need to take to push yourself as a better dancer.

Tip 29: Online classes

Now let's say you're not taking studio classes. Instead, you are watching videos online or taking online courses. Instead of going in person to take intermediate courses, you would go to YouTube or research intermediate-level classes for that specific genre you are doing. Taking classes online will look different than in person; the environment will be different; however, my classes will still challenge your skill level. Depending on what style it is, you can be introduced to new terminology and more advanced moves. For example, suppose you were in ballet. In that case, you might move on from just doing releve in first and second position to learning a chaine turn using those same skills in beginning ballet and advancing from that into intermediate.

Now I know we talked a bit about technique classes and why they are needed. Still, as you advance into more challenging courses, it is essential during this time to make sure that your technique in whatever genre you're moving on from does not fall behind. For example, as people move up levels, their priority shifts from focusing on their technique and the foundation of their dance style to learning more challenging choreo. They want to perform better, and the foundations and techniques get pushed to the back of their head. So it is essential more now than before to make sure you were regularly in technique classes or working on your technique so that when you are learning new skills, you don't have to backtrack to the foundation.

Tip 30: Remembering foundations

Intermediate should be challenging for you. However, if it is too challenging or you see yourself falling backward with your technique or your foundation, it is OK to go back to or take an additional beginner class. There is always something you can learn being in a beginner class, whether that is from the choreographer or focusing on your technique, your expression, performance, etc.

So I encourage you to continue beginner classes while taking intermediate because it is an excellent way to see the difference between a beginner and a middle class. For example, suppose the intermediate class is too challenging for you. In that case, you still have a beginner class where you can focus on your foundations and technique and not necessarily worry about getting the choreo done. That way, you balance challenging choreo and working on your expression performance with what you already know how to do.

Tip 31: Picking up faster

One of the last tips I have for you to be a better dancer or choreographer is challenging yourself to pick up choreography faster. By taking many different choreographers' classes or learning different styles, you'll notice that each teacher teaches at a different pace. For example, some teachers will demonstrate the choreo first, go over the count very slowly, and drill the choreo, so the repetition gets in our minds. At the same time, other choreographers may teach the choreo, go over it with music, run through it a few times, and then move on right away.

You are most likely fine with the more intermediate and advanced choreographers moving quicker in class. As a dancer, this challenge is to see how quickly you retain choreography and push that into your muscle memory while learning additional things. I would recommend practicing choreography quicker by doing it on your own time; I would see if I can learn a piece or combo under a specific time limit. So let's say a standard combo class is about an hour or an hour and 15 minutes. We will spend about 45 minutes learning the combo, taking time to stretch and time for a performance. So what I would do is see if I can learn a piece in under 45 minutes; I would set a timer on my phone and get started.

Tip 32: Observing and apply

Another way to challenge yourself to see if you pick up choreography quickly is to watch it and see if you can pick it up just from your observation instead of having someone teach it to you. It was actually how I started dancing as I watched several YouTube videos of dancers from Millennium Dance Complex LA. These classes did not necessarily have tutorials for me on YouTube, so I would watch them do it repeatedly and see if I could pick up the choreo. Over time as I have become a better dancer and taken classes in the studio, I now always time myself. Watching other people dance and trying to learn it, how quickly I can do that, and how fast I can remember it and get it in my muscle memory.

Tip 33: No mirror

The challenge of dancing away from the mirror pushes you to see if you know the choreography by dancing with your back towards the mirror. Our bodies can get a little tricky when we get used to dancing in front of a mirror. We remember it as we see it instead of just memorizing it based on the movements of our body to the music. So how I would challenge you is to learn the peace, go over it, and once you feel comfortable, turn your back towards the mirror and see if your body remembers what to do when the music plays. It may not be something that you would get on your first try, but you can work towards it. You can do this challenge if you are taking classes at the studio, taking courses online, or watching YouTube videos, pretty much in any space.

Summary

Some ways to become a better dancer involve watching yourself dance. Getting a film of yourself, whether at home or in the studio, is a good way for you to study your dancing and find areas that you want to improve. Another way you can be challenged as a dancer is by working with other dancers. Collaboration is huge for improvement because it allows a space for creativity for both artists, and you can feed off each other for energy, motivation, and progress. The next step is something people overlook, and that is improv. It can be challenging for dancers because it involves allowing your creativity to flow through your body without preparing in advance. But having that space and allowing yourself to create freely will enable you to learn different moves and connect more with your body.

The next step for improving your dancing would be storytelling and facials. Using facials and having a story to tell with your choreography makes the piece more exciting, and it makes you as a dancer more entertaining to watch. Adding facials to your dance can be very challenging because you're focusing not only on the moves but also on your face and making sure it matches the story you are telling. Intermediate classes are something that can challenge you more choreography-wise. If beginner combo classes choreography and musicality are getting too simple or easy for you, moving on to intermediate classes would be the best step for you to make to challenge yourself. Lastly, to connect back with facials and storytelling, identifying your character as a dancer is vital to improving your performance and engaging the audience. Your facials and your storytelling should align with the story that you are performing rather than just random actions that you want to do.

Chapter 4: Performance

Tip 34: Consistency

Consistency is required to see improvement in anything you do. For example, if you want to get better at sports, practice it repeatedly; repetition is the key to training. However, we are not just looking at being consistent at dancing but being consistent at everything that we've talked about in dancing. How can you be consistent in taking technique classes? How can you be consistent in practicing facials? How can you be consistently stretching and taking care of your body? And the list goes on. When you begin to take your craft more seriously, you go over this hurdle of trying to balance life and your art, making sure you have time for both.

Tip 35: Scheduling time

We will look at how you can schedule time within your life and day-to-day schedule to work in dance. One of the ways we can do this is by adding stretching or exercises into our routine; whether that is our morning routine or evening routine, it makes it a regular thing. For example, stretching before getting dressed and eating breakfast or stretching right before you get into bed. Another suggestion would be doing releve or eleve while brushing our teeth in the morning or before bed. Maybe at times, you can do both morning and evening. We can look at the breaks that you have. You don't have to use that time to practice choreography or do exercises necessarily but maybe use that time to improv and just have fun with dance. To remember why you love to dance and express yourself through improv.

Becoming a better dancer does not always look like doing something or always practicing but remember to learn things by watching dance.

Tip 36: Schedules vs. carving out time

The importance of scheduling time is it's so easy for us to forget about something we were working on, mainly because we get so busy with work or school and all these other important things that go on during our day-to-day. So this is why we look more at adding dance to your usual schedule versus carving out time and trying to make it work that way. When you have a schedule, it's consistent. It's not one and done; you don't forget about it because it's a part of your typical day. You do it at the same time every day; that does not change.

However, if we look at how you are carving out time, there is no guarantee that you will be able to do it every single day. You will try and dance whenever you can instead of every day. You aren't being consistent with the time you spend on dance. Some days it will be in the morning, other days it will be at night, and some days not at all. There will come days where you are too busy and can't fit it into your schedule, leading you to not dancing at all, and then, over time, you forget about it. When we have a schedule, we work on being disciplined and doing it consistently. Even if at first it looks like you have a checklist of what your schedule will look like because it's hard to remember, at least you have a list of things you are trying to follow daily to make it a habit.

Tip 37: Performance

One of the best ways to challenge yourself as a dancer is by performing on stage or in front of people. There is a different feeling of adrenaline and a different type of pressure that you feel when you're about to perform. It is an excellent test to see if you actually know the choreography. It gives you an opportunity to practice using facials, portraying a character, and being in performance mode. For example, let's say you were performing in front of your friends. Do you feel this different type of pressure because there are people you know, so their thoughts and opinions matter to you? Sometimes that motivates people to dance even better than they have been in rehearsal, and other times it makes people scared.

In comparison, if you're dancing on stage, sometimes the audience or the fact that you know that nobody you recognize will be in the audience is an extra motivator. Other times, because there are so many people, dancers become scared or nervous. These are just some of the challenges you face as you learn to become a performer.

Tip 38: Why performance helps

Performance is one of the stronger ways you can be challenged as a dancer. There are so many ways I can help you, but what we're going to be looking at is how I can make you more confident with your dancing. And how you can practice your stage presence. It is a huge step, I would say, for people who want to take dance more seriously rather than just a hobby. Remember how we talked about practicing dancing in front of the camera and watching yourself on film?

Well, just like that, performing on stage is another challenge for you. When it comes down to performance time, are you mentally ready? Do you remember the choreography? Do you give your best for this performance, or are you a little shakier? There are a few ways you can go about performing; one of the best ways I recommend is if it's your first time is performing as a group with other people. It helps a lot with the mindset that not everyone is staring at me, but they're staring at us as a team, so if I mess up, it's OK; I don't have the pressure of everyone just looking at me. It can be a small group such as three or six and all the way up to larger groups with over 15 people.

Tip 39: Performance as a group

I recommend performing as a group because it helps with the nerves someone may have for their first performance. If you're performing with other people and it's something that scares you, know that you were not doing it alone. Also, sometimes the dancers you're dancing with may have already performed in front of people before, so they can help you with any questions or concerns you may have or may be able to share some tips if you're nervous before going out on stage. Finally, being a part of a team strengthens you as a dancer because you know you're surrounded by people who have the same interests as you and are there to support you.

 As you do something new for the first time or something that might scare you, it is good to know that you have a supportive family around you to be there for you as you do it. When you get on stage, you can always look to one of them to calm your nerves to remind you that you're not alone. You can count on each other to bring the energy and feed off of each other's energy while performing. Being surrounded by close friends on stage can draw a better performance out of you. If you see your friend giving 110%, you automatically want to push yourself to give 110%. If you see your friend is very energetic and using facials and really into the plies, it's a reminder for you to do the same. We kind of chatted about this in the past but collaborating with other dancers is huge specifically for those reasons. Not only do you have a surrounding of people who can challenge you and support you while they are on the path doing the same thing, but in the end, you guys as a group will become better dancers but better performers.

Tip 40: Performing a solo

 Now performing a solo challenges you in so many different ways. First, you cannot rely on anyone if you forget choreography; second, you have to set the tone for yourself and bring your own energy; you don't have other people to bounce off of unless it's the audience. Third, most people's nerves tend to be a lot stronger when they know that they're performing by themselves, which sometimes leads them to forget choreography right before going on or in the middle of the piece. Although those are some challenging things you will face as a performer going solo, there are also some things you can learn and overcome through this as well.

Such as having the confidence to go and perform; whether it's your best or not, you're still going for it, and you're not relying on anyone else. Sometimes doing a solo is a stepping stone for you. Maybe it was something you thought you could never do, but you were just proving to yourself that you are more than capable of doing some things that scare you. One thing that I've learned from doing a solo depends on the situation, and if someone else helped you with the choreography, nobody knows the choreo except for you. So if you mess up or forget the choreography, nobody else will know except for you.

It provides a place for you to practice your facials during this time. Especially in the scenario of if you forget the choreography, you don't want the audience to know that. So staying strong and remaining calm in your facials will help you through that. When or if you forget the choreography, this is just another opportunity for you to work on your improv. Whether you are performing as a group or a solo, there is always something you can learn and always something that you can work on through your performance.

Tip 41: Choreograph

Challenging yourself as a dancer goes beyond what you can do physically with your body and leans towards what you can do with your mind in the form of creating. Choreographing, I feel, is an overlooked area in the importance of becoming a better dancer. Nowadays, we see dancers always taking classes and performing, but we don't see them teaching a class or choreographing. I feel like choreographing challenges you in originality and being unique. It is a place where your character can come out as well as your choices. So what we first will look at is how to choreograph a piece.

Tip 42: Choreographing a piece

There are several ways you can go about this; you can just pick a song that you're interested in playing and start improving. This is one of the ways to do this if you get stuck on what to do while choreographing. If you have meaning behind this piece, you can start with some research in the sense of what you want this piece to be about, choosing music that fits that concept. If a specific time era surrounds it, what type of moves are used during that time. But before identifying your song, you're going to want to identify your style. I know earlier we talked about what type of dancing you wanted to shoot for, if that is jazz or ballet or contemporary or hip-hop; knowing what type of dance you were trying to become better at was the start, along with your inspiration. So when it comes to choreography, he would want to do the same thing.

 Who or what is your inspiration for this combo? What type of style dance are we doing? is there a message or story we are trying to tell within this piece? What research do I need? What type of music do I need? These little details are the foundation before creating a piece. Even within doing an upbeat hip-hop combo, dancers typically share the meaning behind this piece. Whether it's you're in the middle of a dance circle, and it's your turn to show off, and that is the meaning behind a piece or if it's from a scene and step up, and dance is a form of expression to show why they need the community that they do and to fight for their homes. Each piece has an inspiration and a story.

Next, you're going to want to find a song that you are interested in choreographing that either catches your eye or fits the storyline and what the piece is about. Once you've been able to find the song, the next step would just be getting up and moving. Improv is one of the best ways of choreographing something because no one forces your moves; it's what comes naturally to you. Something that really helps me when I'm choreographing is not necessarily always dancing physically, but imagining what I would do to this part of this song and imagining what move it connects, and just sitting and listening to the music.

Tip 43: Listening to the music

This stuff is something a more intermediate or advanced choreographer would do, just sitting and listening to the music. Understand what type of instruments are being used how they're being used. Be able to count 8-counts within music, identify the easiest way musicality wise to hear that, and listen to the under beats, the under-snare drums, the end counts, and identify that within the music. It would help tremendously if you were able to hear and understand what is going on musically. It makes it ten times easier for you to choreograph it. You'll be able to choreograph to the 8-counts that are easier to hear within the music and then challenge yourself; you can identify and choreograph to the end counts in the under-snare drums that are a little bit harder to hear. The more you become a better listener within the music, the stronger your choreography will be. You'll be able to listen to things within the music that others won't at first, and that will make your choreography and your pieces stand out. It will make your choreography more unique and more challenging to you.

Tip 44: Connect the story

If your piece is more about a specific time or era, this is the time where you would look at incorporating specific moves used during that time. In addition to doing what feels natural, you would want to make sure your actions correspond with the story. However, for example, if you were doing a Halloween theme, your movements wouldn't be, for the most part, elegant and fun, but they would be creepier and scarier. So they would fit the theme of your story and will be able to match the music.

Something that you'll see is everything that we've talked about all goes together. Identifying the instruments is going to, musicality-wise, help your choreography. Your choreography and your facials and characters go hand-in-hand with telling a story. So as we dive more into becoming a better dancer or a better choreographer, we begin to realize that it's not just about the moves. It is about the meaning behind the moves, the inspiration, or the motives. It's about how clearly you can translate that to the audience, not just through your movement but through the storytelling of the music, the dance moves, the facials, and the choices that the dancer makes. They all go hand-in-hand with each other, and I will look at the answers today. Some only focus on specific things, such as mastering the moves. However, they struggle to tell a story.

Dance is more than just about what you can and can't do physically; but it's about telling a story through your movements instead of words. It's about touching people and expressing yourself to the best of your ability. Not necessarily about if you are in advanced classes or if you're able to pick up choreography quickly and have the most flexibility. These are all great things, but they will not be what identifies you as a great dancer. There is so much more behind dancing than just the movements.

Tip 45: Teach the combo

Choreographing a dance and performing is one thing; however, teaching is another. So the next step to making yourself an even better dancer and performer is being able to teach the choreo you came up with. Whether that is teaching your friends, teaching younger people, or teaching a class, you can learn from being in the teacher's point of view. You get a first-hand view of watching people add their own styles and personalities to the choreography.

You teach, and then you get to watch, and sometimes your students inspire you. You'll learn to meet the students where they're at. For example, let's say you are a more advanced dancer than the students you're teaching, and explaining choreography to them using terminology is a bit confusing because they just aren't quite there. Yet, you can relate the choreography to things they may recognize from their life experiences. For example, let's say you're teaching young kids, like toddlers; they may be too young to understand the terminology and what that means.

 Let's say you're trying to get them to put their arms in ballet's first position. They may not be able to recognize the terminology first position and what that means, but if you say OK, now hold a beach ball, they would be able to put their arms in that position. Then slowly, over time, you can connect the position of a beach ball to ballet's first position and teach that to them. You may not be teaching young kids, but this was just an example. For you, as a teacher, your job is to meet the students who were there and teach from there. You cannot have the student doing double pirouette turns when they're still learning to do a single. Sometimes, what that looks like is altering your choreography in a way that still challenges them, but it's closer to where they're at, so they're not overwhelmed. Do not teach a beginner class intermediate or advanced skills when they are not ready.

Tip 46: Explaining the choreography

It is easier to explain choreography to someone who has either danced before or already knows the choreography. However, let's say you're teaching a class of people who are not as familiar with dance and don't know the choreography. You, as a teacher, have to break down the steps not only in a way that explains the movements but in a way that makes sense to the dancer. Using the terminology example, if you say passé and the dancer doesn't know what that is, the move will never be performed. However, if you broke it down to bend your right leg and bring your toe to touch the inside of your left knee, and demonstrate that; the dancer will better understand what you are saying. The imagery you are displaying may help the dancer make a connection from what they just did and remembering that as a passé. Each student and their skill level are sometimes different. In addition to breaking things down in a way that makes sense to them, you will need to demonstrate so the dancer can see what you mean and then be able to try it for themselves.

Chapter 5: Inspiration for being a better choreo

Tip 47: Study the Music

When it comes to choreography, you want to understand the materials you were working with. I have seen several combo classes or teachers talking about the music. They are not just talking about beats that are easier to hear, but about under beats that people may easily miss. They discuss and understand what instruments are being used and how they are used. I know the music that they are working with. So the first thing we're going to look at when we're at that stage of becoming a better choreographer is studying music.

Tip48: Studying the music

What instrument does the song you chose use? Slow it down and figure out what instruments are used in a piece, see when they are being used and how they are being used.

Tip 49: Identifying instruments

Let's say we are focusing on the snare drum, and in one section of this song, the snare is hitting 8-counts, another area of the song it's 4-counts, and the third is 16. We want to be able to identify when the beat switches. We want to see what the pace between a 4-count beat and a 16-count beat sounds like. We also then choose if this is what we want the primary bit of our choreography for you to be on. If we are doing a hip-hop piece, it would be very easy to focus on the snare or the bass drum, just the hard-hitting beats. However, if we are doing a jazz routine and like how our song, in addition to drums, has a lot of trumpets in it, we wouldn't just look at the drums, but we would also look at the way that the trumpet is being used, what that sounds like, and what it looks like with the choreography.

Tip 50: Study music

Another interesting thing you can find when studying music is seeing how specific artists or songs use similar instruments and beats that match their style. So, for example, a song or several songs by Michael Jackson are very much different than Shawn Mendes. Still, when you listen to Michael Jackson's different types of songs, you can identify the reuse of specific instruments or use of particular beats that make you automatically think, oh, this has Michael Jackson feels.

Tip 51: Freestyle

Let's say you have already done your research as to what type of piece you're doing, the era, and the storyline. My tip for you would be to play the music and just listen and improvise. Many choreographers get stuck on what move to start with initially, or maybe they have been choreographing for a bit but don't know what to do next. Improv is one of the best ways to get started or get the juices flowing. With improv, you do what naturally comes to you and your body based on what you already know about your piece and by listening to the music.

Tip 52: Visually improv

Sometimes you can improve what you're physically doing by closing your eyes and imagining. For example, let's say you're choreographing for a group of people, and the counts to this theatrical section within the music that you're not sure what to do about it. This is when imagining your improv comes into play. Maybe you visualize a lift happening here. Perhaps you see ripples happening or dramatic floor work. Sometimes it's easier to visualize it while improving rather than doing it. But, overall, improv gives you the space and the creativity to choreograph your piece based on how you feel when listening and visualizing the music.

Tip 53: Inspiration

Like dancing, one of the foundational steps in choreography is finding inspiration. Find your motivation for wanting to be a choreographer in general, for each piece you do, and for each song you pick. Here are some things you can do if you want to be a choreographer. Ask yourself, why do you want to be a choreographer? What type of dancer do you want to be? Who inspires you to do choreography?

Tip 54: Your why

One of the first things you want to ask yourself is why you want to be a choreographer. Who or what inspires you to want to do this? Like we talked about, inspiration, in the beginning, can come from anyone or anything. Maybe it's because you want to challenge yourself and be more than just a dancer. It could be because you have so many ideas that you just really want to share them. It could be a specific choreography for inspiring you to create your own dances. There could be several reasons as to who inspires you. Once you identify who, you will move on to identifying why. Why does a specific person or thing inspire you? Maybe it's not a particular person; perhaps it's multiple things, but identifying who and why are massive steps to finding out why you want to be a choreographer and your motives behind it.

Tip 55: *Your style*

The next step for you is if you want to start choreography. Start making a piece your own; you can even go the route of reading your own style or combining styles. For example, it could look like a jazz-funk class, which is the color of jazz and hip-hop. You don't have to stick to one specific way; there is no right and wrong way of choreographing either. These are just some suggestions or tips for you to take as you become a choreographer.

Tip 56: *Confidence*

It is your creativity, so you want to be confident in your work. Be secure in who you are as a choreographer; be confident in the choices that you make. Be confident in the story you choose to tell; if you're not confident in your work and creating it, nobody else it's going to be. There are times where you will feel nervous, especially in sharing your choreography for the first time. Your first time may not be your best, and that's OK because being a choreographer is not something you can master, and there's always a learning process. You are always learning new styles, new moves, new storylines, and you're learning from your students.

Chapter 6: Storytelling

Tip 57: Bring to life

After spending time brainstorming and researching what you want to bring to life, you've started to create. Whether it's in your mind or you have it on paper, start putting it into place instead of just thinking about it. I feel there are a lot of choreographers who have great ideas in their minds and great concepts but never had the confidence to step out and bring them to life. So if you have a specific song and a particular move that you know you want to do within the piece, start physically practicing that. Start playing the music you chose, and maybe there were specific moves that you liked when you were improving or visualizing. Start putting that together and adding it to the piece. Figure out which move you want to do first and then do what naturally comes next after that.

Tip 58: Chunking

An easier way for your mind to process the choreography with the music is chunking. Choreograph by sections instead of doing the whole thing simultaneously and throwing it all together. For example, let's say, in your mind, you visualize some floor work, but you also have a choreography set that you created during improv that is more outstanding. So you have two separate sections that you can chunk and then figure out how you want to blend them later. For example, how does the dancer go from standing up to getting to the floor to do the floor work, and then how do they transition after that? When you start choreographing and chunking, you don't necessarily have to start at the beginning of the song or the beginning of your starting place for the piece. Sometimes starting it in the middle or towards the end is easiest when choreographing.

Tip 59: Drill the chunks

Once you have choreography chunked into specific sections, you then want to start drilling the choreography. Make sure you know what section goes with what part of the song within the music. and let's go back to the example of you needing to find a transition from standing up to the floor work. After drilling the choreography doing both chunk sections, you then just want to improv the in-between space and see what comes naturally. Just like improving to create a piece when you're stuck and need a move or a transition, improv can help you there.

Tip 60: Research ideas

Another suggestion I have for when you're stuck in choreography is to research. For example, if you need a transition move from standing to floor and you really can't think of anything or feel anything that comes naturally, you can always research to give you some ideas on creating your own move. I believe researching ideas is not something choreographers necessarily look at, but it can be beneficial, especially if you are stuck.

Tip 61: Era

If you were doing a piece on a specific era as a choreographer, you would need to research the type of music and maybe some popular dance moves and how they danced during that particular era. You would need to do this because you would be unfamiliar with the dance moves at the time, and you'll need some inspiration. The same thing applies when you are stuck in choreography and can't figure out what to do next; researching is always a way to find inspiration.

Tip 62: Formations

Now formations are huge when it comes to storytelling. Formations allow choreographers to create visuals, not just to tell the story but also to use the space in the visuals to tell a story. There are always formations, whether it is one dancer or 15 dancers. Formation focuses on the spacing and where a dancer may move within the piece. If in bigger groups, the formation can allow for effects and ripples and just a place to let the choreographer get more creative. Now you can only do waves and things along that line when you are with a group of dancers; however, there are still ways you can apply formation to create a nice visual when it is only one dancer.

Tip 63: Formations for solos

The difference between doing formations for solos and a group is not as different as you may think. Formations just focus on where the dancer will move in that moment. Yes, when you have a group of people, they allow you to set this visual up for your piece; however, formation still applies when working with just one dancer. We will continue the example of working on the transition from standing to floor work. If a dancer is transitioning from standing to the ground, maybe your transition can do something that allows the dancer to move. For example, you could do a Jasmine slide and do that forward, so the dancer's transition to the ground while moving to a different location creates this formation. Let's say you are doing a jazz routine, and you have pirouettes and leaps and jumps.

You would not want to do this all-in-one spot but rather have the dancer use the space given to dance the solo. So maybe you have pirouettes being done stage left, and then you have leaps that carry you over to stage right where your jumps will be. This is an example of formation because the dancer is moving from different locations, and what makes it a formation is because it's choreographed that way. The choreographer made jumps to the stage right and pirouettes stage left. The choreographer made the leaps as a transition between different formations for the dancer.

Tip 64: Group Formations

Now with group formations, the choreographer has complete freedom to place the dancers wherever they need to be and through that be able to create this visual or this effect for the audience to enjoy. There are so many different ways you can place your dancers you can have them be in two parallel lines and do ripples down the line. You can have a V shape formation with the tip of the V and the center of the dancer being downstage closer to the audience creating a ripple that way from the very tip of the V in the front to the back and another suggestion you can do is clumps. These different formations especially with groups allow you to be more creative. So let's say you separated your 15 dancers into three groups you clumped one group stage left a second group stage right and the third group in the center. To challenge yourself as a choreographer you could have the two side groups both stage left and stage right doing different choreography than the group and stage center but in a way that complements them so that visually it can make the piece look more interesting and more exciting to the audience. you could then learn how to highlight and storytelling within the formations.

Tip 65: Storytelling in formations

In addition to what we were talking about before of doing separate choreography to complement centerstage, you could add specific lifts or tricks within the piece at particular moments that highlight the dancers. In any sort of storytelling, there is rising action, climax, and there's a downfall. Dancing, we want to keep the storytelling exciting and interesting for the audience so maybe have climactic points within the dance that draw the audience's attention and highlight the dancers. It can be done through formations, ripples, lifts, tricks, or highlighting dancers. The challenge comes in between his highlighting moments; we don't want the choreography to go downhill and be more boring to watch. But the ultimate goal is to be able to tell your story while constantly having new attention grabbers within the routine so that the dance does not become boring for the audience to watch but is more exciting and interesting.

Tip 66: Execution

When we talk about execution, we're looking at how well your performance and choreography are to the storyline you want to tell. How are the formations in comparison to how you imagined them to be? Does the visual and the overall dance tell the story you wanted it to tell? Does it give you or the audience the feeling that you wanted? These are questions that you want to ask yourself as you get towards the end of your piece. Will you start wrapping up the choreography? Is it what you wanted as a choreographer? Are your dancers executing it to the best of their ability? If you didn't know what the story was about, would you be able to watch the dance and understand what the message of the story was?

Tip 67: Delivering the message

An excellent way to check and see if the story was told and if the choreography was good is to get an outsider's opinion. Have other dancers and choreographers watch your choreography and ask them to give honest feedback. It is a great way to see if the storyline was told because they come in and have no idea what the story is about, so if they can understand it, then the audience will understand. Specifically, having other dancers come in, they will be able to look at the choreography and relate to it in the sense of knowing if it was done well or not, or see if there are areas that need fixing or better technique.

Tip 68: Check with dancers

Lastly, one of the things you're going to want to do is check with your dancers. See if the choreography or the musicality makes sense to them, or if they have any questions or things that they just don't understand, you will address that. As a choreographer, you are also a teacher as, in a way, you are teaching the choreography to them. So this is a learning opportunity for you not just as a choreographer but also as a teacher to see if you taught in a way that they understood. If certain areas are grey and not only one dancer struggled with, but maybe multiple struggled with, then you know that area needs to be your primary focus on drilling and nitpicking and fixing.

The relationship between your dancers should be mutual, and as you teach them the choreography, they should be able to respond and help you as a teacher by addressing specific problems they may have or areas they need to work on. Maybe it is just how you explain something as a teacher that didn't make sense to the dancers. So as a choreographer, you can take that and look at the way you teach and see if there's anything you want to do differently, that may help the dancers understand more than your previous teaching methods.

Summary

Storytelling goes beyond just the movements and dance. It goes by showing your creative side as a choreographer. To expand beyond choreography and apply visuals in your piece, and have the opportunity to play around with different formations. Use research on specific eras and apply specific moves to your choreography to see how that takes the story to the next level. Bringing in outside opinions can be beneficial to make sure your stories are getting across clearly, such as bringing other dancers or other choreographers. As they share a common interest in dance, they may be able to give some helpful tips as to making your piece stronger or more understandable for an audience. If other dancers or choreographers can understand what the work is about without knowing anything from the start, it is a good sign that you are doing an excellent job with the story.

In addition to getting advice from other people, you want to check in with your dancers and see how they comprehend the dance and story. Does it make sense to them as you teach it to them? Are they understanding the piece and choreography, and are they understanding the character they need to play to bring a story to life? There are many little details beyond dancing that go into the elements of telling a story as a choreographer. These little details don't seem like much to worry over, but they'll make a big difference in your performance both as a dancer and a choreographer.

Chapter 7: Review

Tip 69: Review the fundamentals

Inspiration, what is your inspiration? Who or what inspires you to do what you love?

There is a need for inspiration because it motivates you to do what you want to do. Did you want to ration of dance do you create? Even on those days when you don't feel like working on your craft, it gives you something to push you to do it. If your inspiration is a person, it gives you someone to look up to when it comes to how you should train, who you should train with, and what your style is.

Inspiration as a choreographer is the foundational step when it comes to choreographing. What is your piece about? What mood or feeling are we trying to portray, and why? These detailed questions about inspiration help make your performance better and more meaningful.

Tip 70: On the floor

Take your inspiration to the dance floor, knowing how your inspiration motivates you to be a better dancer or choreographer. If you see how someone you look up to in dance stretches and workouts, they maybe apply that to your routine. If music is your inspiration, use the opportunity to choreograph to the music and practice dancing and moving to what you love. It's watching those who inspire you and allowing them to affect your life and your development as a dancer.

Tip 71: Don't miss a warm-up

Warming up is essential to being a dancer, no matter what level you are. Taking care of your body by warming up protects yourself from any injuries and allows you to practice to the best of your ability. Warming up is not just a protective action, but it can further you as a dancer by pushing your flexibility. If you work on your splits every day, eventually mastering a split won't be too far off. In addition, it keeps your muscles loose for dancing and strong for other skills you are trying to learn.

Tip 72: Styles in the warm-up

There are several different ways to warm up. The only thing needed is to stretch all elements of your body from head to toe, not just some. You can warm up stationary or while moving; both can be effective. One thing you want to look out for while warming up is identifying what areas on your body are tighter than others. Those tighter areas are the areas you may want to hold the stretch longer and could be at risk for injuries while dancing.

Tip 73: Fundamentals

No matter what dance style you decide to pursue, fundamentals are always needed. The fundamentals of ballet are at the foundations of all types of dances, so I recommend starting there. However, as you move more into your style, there are additional fundamental classes that you would want to learn. For example, if you wanted to focus on musical theatre dance, you would want to take jazz fundamentals, tap fundamentals, ballet, hip hop, contemporary, modern, and more to be trained as a musical theatre dancer. On the other hand, maybe you just want to focus on jazz, then you would take jazz fundamentals in addition to ballet.

Tip 74: Repetition of fundamentals

Even if you are an advanced dancer, you still need the fundamentals and foundations. As you develop into more advanced classes and become a better dancer, you still need to review the basics. The reason why is as you become a better dancer and learn new skills, you don't want the skills you already know to get weak or sloppy because you will need this to develop as a dancer. For example, if you are ready for a triple pirouette turn but your releve is dropping, then you need to go back to singles or doubles. Doing a triple pirouette turn on a low releve can cause injuries as you are turning. In addition to that, if you want to go beyond a triple, with a low releve, your balance will be off, making it difficult for you to go further.

Tip 75: Your style

Identifying your style identifies what type of dance you would want to do. It is because there are so many different styles, and you don't necessarily only have to do one. However, for the sake of becoming a better dancer, choose the type of dance you want to focus on.

You then would apply what you already know to that style, doing jazz technique and fundamentals classes if your style is jazz— understanding ballet fundamentals if you are more on the route of pursuing ballet.

Tip 76: Different styles

There is an importance in being familiar with various styles; as you become a better dancer, you want to expand to different types because they all can interloop with each other. So, for example, looking back at the foundations of ballet, it is the foundation for all dance styles. You will see the ballet in contemporary, jazz, and hip hop. So if you were going to practice jazz and want to improve in that, you will also be learning ballet terminology and its foundations.

Tip 77: Your beat

Now that you have your style, you want to find your beat. One of the ways I recommend doing this is through improv. Dancing to music and just having fun within the style of your interest. Identifying the beats with the music, hitting those beats with your body, and making that connection is one of the first hurdles.

Someone who does not have a dance background may struggle with throwing themselves into combo classes and choreography. Just feeling the music and finding that beat is the first challenge. Finding your beat should not be stressful; it should be a fun environment where you can improvise to the beat to find your rhythm.

Tip 78: Understanding the music

Finding your beat requires listening to the music and understanding what is happening. Being able to see and understand what instruments are being used and how they are being used helps you understand the sounds they make.

Listening to the music can also help you identify the 8-counts within the piece to see what beats you want to hit. You can see where the music speeds up and where it's slowed down. With identifying that, you can then apply it to the body, how you want to dance, and when you want to dance that way.

Tip 79: Technique

The technique is essential not just as an advanced dancer but even as a beginner. When you learn the basic techniques in your dance style, it helps you to be able to expand as a beginner dancer. It, in a way, gives you guidelines to developing into a better dancer and a stronger dancer.

Tip 80: Types of technique

There are several different technique classes you can take, and in these classes, you can learn the basics; whether you take online or in-person courses, both offer a learning opportunity for you. For example, if you were to take ballet technique, you would learn how to do foundational dance moves and terminology that you may run across in other classes.

Tip 81: Difference between technique

In the example of ballet technique classes, you will learn the basic five positions. You will learn how to hold a proper releve and eleve. You will learn how to maintain a proper passe and build the strength within your legs so you can develop into learning how to do a pirouette, how to do pique turns, and how to leap across the floor.

Tip 82: Beginner combo

Beginner combo classes challenge you in so many different ways. You go from dancing at home to dancing in class, from dancing alone to dancing in an environment with other dancers. You no longer are going at your own pace when learning a combo, but you are going at the teacher's pace. You now have the opportunity to ask questions in person with a teacher in class. It challenges you in learning from a teacher you may not be familiar with.

Tip 83: Choreography in class

Beginner classes allow you to focus on choreography instead of just on technique. You concentrate on how quickly you can pick up choreography if you are ready to be in combo classes. Combo classes also challenge you in the sense of working with a teacher in person. How do you work with specific people, and is this teacher teaching in a way you understand?

Tip 84: Bounce off the energy

Beginner combo classes also allow you to dance with groups. You dance with other dancers and feel the energy for the first time. Seeing how well you dance with other dancers or dance in front of people for the first time. Another thing you can learn as you take beginner combo classes is retaining the choreography. Do you remember what moves come first and last without watching other people? When performing in groups, you want to stray away from needing to watch other dancers for choreography. Rather just focus on what you know and what you remember. Lastly, combo classes are good for challenging yourself to get out of your comfort zone. Instead of dancing at home, you have a studio class you can take where you have the opportunity to meet other dancers and challenge yourself to learn in a new environment.

Tip 85: Importance of repetition

Like any sport, repetition is vital for building muscle memory and dance. However, you don't just need the repetition of dancing every day but doing specific skills every day. The repetition of dancing every day gets you in the habit of practicing more than just a few times a week. It also allows you to see how you develop in dancing. Typically doing a repetition of the specific style you're going for helps you become a stronger dancer in that area. For example, when you are practicing your elevation, the stronger your calves become, the easier your calves will be able to hold you while you're doing pirouettes and pique turns. Another area we can look at is the repetition needed for stretching, not just stretching a few times a week, but stretching every day and seeing the difference within your flexibility. When you push yourself to stretch daily, you're setting yourself up for success when trying new skills or new styles. You will be prepared for it, and your body will be capable of doing it if your flexibility is where it's needed to be.

Tip 86: Making a schedule

To have repetition with your dancing, you need to create or have a schedule. What time during your day is best for you to focus on dance? Whether it's once a day or twice a day, it's crucial that you find the time to dedicate to dance. It is much easier to do it at the same time every day so that it can become a part of your daily routine. Some other options are just planning what works for you, depending on that day.

Tip 87: Plan

In addition to the schedule, you want to have some sort of idea as to what area you want to work on when you're practicing dance. For example, maybe in the morning, you focus on stretching and exercising your muscles. Whereas in the evening, you can concentrate on choreography that you may have learned or improv. Making it a habit of every morning, you're focusing on strengthening and getting stronger as a dancer, and in the evening, you look at retaining choreography or improving. This way, it is repetition as to what you're working on at a specific time, and it becomes part of your routine.

Tip 88: observation

There's are some important things you can learn from watching other dancers. You can see their choices, how they dance, and how they are hitting moves compared to yourself. When doing this, you have to be careful not to observe other dancing in the sense of comparison but rather in a way that can push you to be more creative with your choices.

Tip 89: Watch in class

Some ways you can watch other dancers is in person or through video. In class, while other people are doing groups and it's their time to perform, watch them to see the choices they make, and is there anything you like that they did and maybe something you didn't like that they did. It is a learning opportunity for you, and you can use what you like and apply that to your performance. It is a time where you can see if it's something you like or feel comfortable with while dancing. It is a time for you to explore and see some different ways you can hit a move, explore your options, and figure out what works best for you.

Tip 90: YouTube

Another way is by watching videos online. There are many videos online of dancers dancing from different studios, under various choreographer names, and more. When watching dancers online, you can watch and take notes about their performance on camera. In addition, you can watch how the choices they make are performed on film. Lastly, since it is on the video, you can replay the videos and dive deeper into their performance.

Tip 91: Character within performance

Although we are focusing on dance, character development and acting are heavily involved. When you are dancing and putting on a performance, you want to have a story you are telling. Within that story, you need to have characters, a timeline, a conflict, and a detailed background that goes into telling your story. For example, if we're doing a piece about the musical Hairspray set in the 60s, not just physical appearance would play a role in the story, but the way the dancers are moving and some of the styles. If you're dancing a meaningful story or just a story in general, the performers will need to be more than dancers to portray the story. They need to embrace it by adding specific facials and character choices.

Tip 92: Storytelling

When telling a story through dance, like any other way of expressing this, would require research. What is this piece about, what do they wear, how do they talk, how do they dance, and what dance moves were used during that era? These are essential things to apply to your performance, allowing the dancers to take on the characters of the story you're trying to portray.

Tip 93: Understanding

Lastly, from the dancer's perspective, do you understand the story? Do you know what this piece is about? If you struggle to understand what the work is about, you will struggle to portray it to the audience. Understanding the characters is key for the performance, whether you are a dancer or an actor, or any other entertainer. If you don't understand the character, he won't be able to portray it well; therefore, the audience won't understand the character either. The dancers must explore what that character means to them and apply their facials, different choices in the performance, and the routine that complements the story and compliments them as a dancer.

Tip 94: Becoming a better dancer

No matter what level you are at, there are always areas you can improve. A key factor in improving yourself as a dancer is watching yourself dance. Whether you're at home or in the studio, getting a film of yourself dancing and watching it is vital for you to see what areas you want to improve on and see growth between where you are now and where you were when you started. Some combo classes will have a person come in and film the class with their camera so you can have access to that through them, and sometimes you may just have to ask a stranger to film you on your phone, and that's okay too. As long as you get in the habit of filming and seeing yourself on film, you'll be able to set goals as to what areas you want to work on just based on watching yourself perform. The same thing applies if you were taking online classes or dancing at home; set up your phone and videotape yourself to have footage to look back on to see the improvement.

Tip 95: Collaboration

Another key to becoming a better dancer is by working with other dancers. And, in classes when they film you, sometimes you are filmed in groups to make you a bit more comfortable dancing in front of the camera. Also, it is an excellent opportunity for you to get to know and meet other dancers. Dancing with other people and having a group of people who share the same passion as you help keep you on track when it comes to your motivation, as well as you guys can challenge each other to become stronger dancers.

Tip 96: Learning from others

Working with other people allows you to learn from others, get some of your ideas, and be creative when it comes to choreography. Having a group of people or more than one person who also loves dance helps you stay focused on why you are doing what you love. And it's more fun to do with the good people than by yourself. Not only is it good for you and your improvement to surround yourself with dancers who are just as good or maybe even better than you, but it's also more fun when you have a challenge and don't have to go through this period of learning how to dance alone.

Tip 97: More advance

As the beginning classes become too easy for you, intermediate classes would be a good option to keep yourself challenged—no matter what style you're doing. For example, if you're doing ballet but also taking jazz classes, and jazz is getting way too easy for you; however, ballet is still a struggle for you; it's okay for you to stay in beginner ballet while you move into intermediate jazz. One thing to remember as you advance in classes is not to forget the basics in the foundation. Once you go onto intermediate classes with more intermediate skill level combinations and moves, it is key for you to remember the foundations and the technique to make sure you are prepared and capable of doing these skills. Intermediate classes differ from beginner classes because they offer a more advanced choreography, the teacher may go at a faster pace, and musicality is slightly different. In beginner classes, the musicality is very easy to hear the 8-counts, and when the beat is. In contrast, in intermediate class, you may be challenged to hear different rhythms within the music; it may not always be easy to hear, but to identify it and see that it's there is the challenge of being in an intermediate class.

Tip 98: Pick up

If you move into an immediate class and it's too challenging for you, but a beginner is too easy for you, there are some ways you can challenge yourself while still being in a beginner class. One of the ways you can do this is by challenging yourself to pick up choreography faster. It is holding yourself accountable; it's not something that an outside person will force you to do, but it is a good challenge if you are not ready to move up to intermediate but still want to be challenged. Even in beginner classes, there's still something that you can learn and work on, and so one of the things I would recommend is to challenge yourself to pick up choreography faster. You can practice this by doing the choreography facing away from the mirror and away from other people. Sometimes you can even do it with your eyes closed. It forces you to remember the choreography not based on what you see other people doing or what you hear the choreographer saying, but by memory and trying to get your muscle memory to remember and retain the choreography faster.

Tip 99: Inspiration

One of the primary things to remember is that you have to have inspiration for what you're doing or what is the purpose of you becoming a better dancer. Who motivates you? What motivates you? Having that in the back of your mind reminds you every day of what you're doing and why you're doing it; it keeps you accountable for who to look up to when you're learning this craft.

Your inspiration doesn't necessarily have to be a person; it can be music or the specific feeling that you get when you dance. The key thing is to identify that before beginning dancing so that you are not just dancing for fun but for a reason.

Tip 100: Performance

This is not necessary for every dancer but more for people who want to dance and perform. Entertaining the audience is critical when you're performing. Meaning it's not just about the moves and how well you can do them, it's not just about the music, and it's not simply just about the facials and how you can do those. But it's a combination of all of it, and how that affects the audience is what makes an outstanding performance.

Tip 101: Ask yourself

Are you fun to watch? Are you having a good time? It is a combination of things that draws the audience in; you're dancing and the energy that comes with it, the facials, the attitude and storytelling, and the music. Each has a key role in performance; on the dancer's end, it is our job to know the choreography, express the story through our facials, and help portray it through our movements.

Summary

These are just the beginning tips on learning to dance and become a better dancer. In this, we focused on our inspiration, why it's needed, technique, and the difference between styles. We learned where to start learning how to dance, whether in the studio or at home, and how to become a better dancer by challenging yourself in class or taking more intermediate classes. The importance of repetition and a routine for stretching, taking care of your body, and practicing your craft. We looked at ways you can create through improv, collaborating with other dancers, and teaching class. We also looked at performances and what makes a great performance - through facials and storytelling.

About the Expert

Sydney Marie Skipper is a dancer and choreography for hip hop dance and musical theatre. Sydney has been a dancer for 15 years and received training from the Millennium Dance Complex in California. Growing up, she competed at dance competitions; she danced in numerous performances such as Lip Sync Battle on Telemundo and music videos for artists Emilio Roman and Macy Kate. In addition, she worked alongside choreographers who work within the dance industry. Sydney has choreographed anything from quinceaneras, hip hop team performances, children's theatre, and musical theatre at Grand Canyon University. Therefore, she wrote this beginner book for new dancers and choreographers.

HowExpert publishes quick 'how to' guides by everyday experts. Visit HowExpert.com to learn more.

Recommended Resources

- HowExpert.com – Quick 'How To' Guides on All Topics from A to Z by Everyday Experts.
- HowExpert.com/free – Free HowExpert Email Newsletter.
- HowExpert.com/books – HowExpert Books
- HowExpert.com/courses – HowExpert Courses
- HowExpert.com/clothing – HowExpert Clothing
- HowExpert.com/membership – HowExpert Membership Site
- HowExpert.com/affiliates – HowExpert Affiliate Program
- HowExpert.com/jobs – HowExpert Jobs
- HowExpert.com/writers – Write About Your #1 Passion/Knowledge/Expertise & Become a HowExpert Author.
- HowExpert.com/resources – Additional HowExpert Recommended Resources
- YouTube.com/HowExpert – Subscribe to HowExpert YouTube.
- Instagram.com/HowExpert – Follow HowExpert on Instagram.
- Facebook.com/HowExpert – Follow HowExpert on Facebook.
- TikTok.com/@HowExpert – Follow HowExpert on TikTok.

Printed in Great Britain
by Amazon

82819591R00048